REPOINTING

THE

BRICKS

Repointing the Bricks

Jacqueline Bourque

Mansfield Press

Printed in Canada

Library and Archives Canada Cataloguing in Publication

Title: Repointing the bricks / Jacqueline Bourque.
Names: Bourque, Jacqueline, author.
Description: Poems.
Identifiers: Canadiana 20210340312 | ISBN 9781771262736 (softcover)
Classification: LCC PS8603.O95563 R47 2021 | DDC C811/.6—dc23

Editor: Jim Johnstone
Layout & Design: Erica Smith

ONTARIO ARTS COUNCIL
CONSEIL DES ARTS DE L'ONTARIO
an Ontario government agency
un organisme du gouvernement de l'Ontario

Canada Council for the Arts
Conseil des arts du Canada

The publication of *Repointing the Bricks* has been generously supported by the Canada Council for the Arts and the Ontario Arts Council.

Mansfield Press Inc.
25 Mansfield Avenue, Toronto, Ontario, Canada M6J 2A9
Publisher: Denis De Klerck
www.mansfieldpress.net

For my Mother and Father
and for Kim

Contents

1.

2.

3.

4.

1.

Bio

My parents offered me
whitecaps, cordgrass
blonde stretches of beach—

the same shores where
village priests implored
the Blessed Virgin:

Je vous salue Marie

black robes whipping
fishermen back to safety.

I resist placid bays,
shed new homes
like the Northumberland tides,

don't submit
to full disclosure
or ownership—

yet ashore I turn up
as if at my confidant's feet.

This morning the sun
flatters the channel
with a shimmy of sequins

as I sit on the sand and listen.

Landing in the Maritimes

As flight AC 8798 touches down,
something inside my psyche jerks
like a carpenter's plane pushing through
a resistant knot. Then the drive

to Monique and Paul's, my past
darting through the Staghorn Sumacs,
Speckled Alders, Red Osler Dogwoods, Witch Hazels,
and joining the spontaneous happiness
that the surgeon's words lit in me a few days earlier:
It's benign.

I enter their home and seek out
the bliss I imagine occurs
with partnership and children.
Anxiety awaits at another doorway.

At dinner, their son Alex joins us,
a thirty year old who jogs
five kilometres regularly (he has his mother's
defined upper lip). He looks at me
as if searching for clues.

Over bottles of Sauvignon Blanc,
we play armchair psychologist. Then Alex
challenges us: *Come on, admit it,*
you don't have all your shit together.

Cumulus

This morning, figureless clouds
hover over whitecaps.
I pull on a wool turtleneck, brace
for ice as I step out of the trailer.
But no…
                warm wadding,
                wild roses.

At noon, a patch of indigo
bustles through. Southward,
a fringe of mackerel sky
edges an opaque yellow-white
cover. Overhead, overlaying

cerulean, white rachis
and afterfeathers. I have super-
imposed these skies
on all the places I've lived,
gauged wind and light

against Northumberland's rule.
This climate lodges itself
in the marrow—triggers it
with a slight salt breeze,
the whistle of a piping plover.

The Dune as Bookmark

Maman and I walked the dune
the year the boardwalk was built.
A glow had drained from her
yet her arms sashayed
in sync with her skirt.

I wanted to embalm the afternoon.

Until that day, my visits to New Brunswick had calmed
me—my father's way of pushing back
in his arm chair,
the aroma
of my mother's homemade
soups.

On this trip,
the intermittent beep
of a low battery
yanked at my stomach.

Maman needed medication to sleep,
seemed to want to breathe
for my father. She told stories
about her 2 a.m. ambulance calls
when he struggled for breath.

Once, I caught her watching for me
through the stairwell window.
I was back from buying groceries.
My mother, busy
with crossword puzzles
or the accounts for some charity, never
waited for me to arrive.

My brother and I stood by.
Both of us sins of omission.

Straddling the balance of city and dune,
of career and parents,
I had always considered moving back
to Dieppe—

Maman balked at the idea. *No old world servitude*
for my daughter.

She had aborted
business college
and returned to her parents' farm to nurse
her ailing mother.

This was before that walk on the dune,
before her diagnosis.

On my last visit *Maman* insisted
I sleep in her room in the seniors' residence.
The attendants arranged a cot
perpendicular to her
bed. The next morning
she watched
from the lobby as I drove off.

A decade after her death
the dune draws me beyond
the boardwalk's predictability.
I descend the stairs into unchartered
sands, the banks that beckon
me to go beyond
what I see.

Four kilometers in—
            a breach
where a nor'easter heaved
its narrow midriff
into the strait.

But even that is overlooked
as each day
slides into sea.

Aboiteau

Let go at low tide, swing shut at high
embankment and sluice, cribwork and clapper valve
muddy your hands, land of creation
shoulder to shoulder, dig, lift and carry

embankment and sluice, cribwork and clapper valve
years of drainage, centuries of runoff
shoulder to shoulder, dig, lift and carry
farmland below sea level, a shaped identity

years of drainage, centuries of runoff
Acadians—communal and close-knit
farmland below sea level, a shaped identity
borders and distrust, war underfoot

Acadians—communal and close-knit
a resolve to stay out of it, harvests to bring in
borders and distrust, war underfoot
hinged valves unhinged, *maudite guerre!*

a resolve to stay out of it, harvests to bring in
soldiers in red, ships in the bay
hinged valves unhinged, *maudite guerre!*
loss of footing, faceless exodus

soldiers in red, ships in the bay
grains careening, Fundy's blue selvage
loss of footing, faceless exodus
beloved pastures, bountiful bogs

muddy your hands, land of creation
grains careening, Fundy's blue selvage
beloved pastures, bountiful bogs
let go at low tide, swing shut at high.

Lion's Mane Jellyfish

Unmoored, bloom of epidermis and mesoglea
no heart, no brain
an undersea of indifference
that jolts even the smoothest swimmer
into volte-face
as if the sight of these crimson pulsating oases
breaches boreal membranes
and pitches all into their archaic unconscious
where thin margins isolate unresolved
distress, registered, yet unknown   a rupture
triggered by the medusa stage's showy stinging
barbs—Medusa's serpentine mane—
punishment for having been raped.
But in this pelagic world, spontaneous generation
prevails: when Perseus lays her petrifying
head on Ethiopia's shores
Medusa's blood spills onto seaweed
and the Red Sea's
shoreline explodes into a blooming rapture of coral.

Ribes Triste

From our kitchen window over the sink
you could spot the path that wound
its way over hardened snow, leading
to a brick school—
children at play in plain view.

One February day, at lunch, *Maman* stung me
point blank:

Why are you alone during recess?

Until then, during what seemed like interminable
recesses, I kicked snowbanks,
looked from side to side
as if talking
to friends. I pretended
because I imagined my mother
was omnipresent, witnessing my wretched aloneness
as if I were a vacant lot where bitter currants grew.
By her seeing

that day, she found my shame,
what I was secreting
in our yellow painted bungalow,
even from myself.

Saturday Morning

After "My brother comes to me" by Tiphanie Yanique

In a small town, in a small yellow bungalow
the woman, who never cries, weeps
into a chenille bedspread. The man,
who seldom speaks, paces in the mahogany hallway.
The child, who is their child, moves soundlessly
across the bedroom's threshold, her right hand
finding her mother's back
                                        pat… pat…

The child compresses misery, bodily, until it is stone.
Years later, it breaches her perimeter.
Anything to prevent the woman from slipping
into tidewaters, anything to implore the man
to place his hand on the woman's back,
anything to preserve the smallness of Saturday morning.

Brise-lames

They rise above dishevelled marshes
pour le brisement de la mer
like a crew of scullers
trunks leaning past the vertical

At the finish of their drive
lame longue, lame courte
stoic markings that explain the past
futile railings wound through a child's world

Their defiance hatches snow
powdered gusts slip through their gaping breaches
ondulation des eaux sous l'action du vent
like fervent parents, unable to absolutely protect

S'amincit à son sommet, écume et déferle
decayed sentinels, ancient sentries
at dusk, their muzzles point towards sky
ululate, call us by our ancestors' names

After Sunday Mass

After Sunday mass, just before lunch
I went into the back yard
and waved my arms at the sky.
I jumped and twirled, incanting

> *clouds away*
> *winds away*
> *sun, dance on my shoulders*

On summer days
the elements aligned
and cousins, aunts, uncles
formed a fleet
as we headed to the coastline.

If the tide was high, we skipped
over hot sand
and propelled into the surf.

If it was low, we walked shallow pools
losing sight of family
before reaching a swimmable depth.

First in, last out,
my teeth never chattered—

On rare occasions my father waded in
arms raised. When he was waist high,
he'd pause for an eternity, then plunge
into a frantic dog paddle.

He grew up in Scoudouc,
which meant hours to reach the Northumberland.
My mother grew up in Cap-Pelé
a 25-minute horse-ride. During the summer months
she and her siblings
crowded into the family carriage—
no adults—rode to the shores at Trois-Ruisseaux.
They were all swimmers.

After my swim
I walked over to Parlee Beach's public house.
Up the stairs, facing the ocean,
was a canteen, the smell of fries, catsup,
suntan lotion, salt-wet cement.
On the first floor, at shoreline level,
lay an open terrace punctuated with pillars.
A jukebox played *Peggy Sue*
while girls danced with one another.

What skills *Papa* lacked in swimming,
he made up for in toe-stepping to music.
Every weekday at 6:45 am,
he step-danced in our kitchen
to the daily jig aired on CBC radio.
My mother, half awake
at the stove, would twist her mouth
and look away.

A young girl was once seen at Parlee Beach
with a handsome stranger she had just met.
She wore a red flared skirt, halter top
that exposed tanned shoulders.
Her ponytail bopped as they moved
from slow and low, to wild and angular
in sync with the backbeat.
He stepped forward through to a swing move,
pushed her off with one hand,
backed away
vanished.
On her back—four long claw-scratches
dripped blood.

My grandmother, laughing to herself,
wiping her eyes, told me that *Papa*
would arrive after an evening out
and step-heel, heel-step his way
across the kitchen floor, into the pantry.

We sought out *Maman* to deflate devil stories.
Not for the "girl at Parlee" though—
its scarlet crackle
silenced me.

After Sunday mass, my grandmother whispered to me
that in her time, dancing
was considered evil. Priests disapproved.
Gazing through our picture window—

> *Your grandfather and I liked to spin and stomp.*
> *There were house parties*
> *where we swung till midnight.*
> *One evening, leaving our neighbour's house,*
> *we entered into a snowfall—ice crystals so clear*
> *against the black night we could see*
> *their branches. Your grandfather took my hand*
> *and we ran home,*
> *laughing all the way.*

Europa, at Dawn, After the Abduction

Crete's daybreak sows frames of sun
through a louvered roof

March about to unfold
not in the way

other dates have, but with a peeled back freshness,
a fleeting montage

that keeps me awake nights,
the walls of a gorge closing in

preventing me
from fleeing.

Perhaps it's Zeus's smile
how it laps like a wave across his entire face,

the back-of-a-shovel hit
to my consciousness

(I blush at how I reached out to stroke him!)

Zeus gifted me
with a javelin that never misses—

I gaze at the sea
and a mourning song

meanders through as if finding its way
to Hiram's aborted love.

Morning lingers, lavished in wild orchids

and I must decide: refuse Zeus
or let the day drift into whatever it wants to be.

Themis, the Day After the Family Reunion

My brother Steropes' words are a siege
inside my temples,
a brown-grey belt
choking Mount Olympus.

I try to smooth the fabric that drapes my clan—
a cloth they incessantly taint
with their muddied souls.

I will take each sibling aside,
talk to them.

Order will unfold in time.

A dog barks in agreement.

My blood relations
arrive late or not at all
            (when they show up, they aren't present)
attain success but never thrive.

Our ancestors, Aether and Hemera
dethroned their parents, a betrayal
that plaited manic threads
into us, inflicted us with rivalry.

Clotho, my daughter, says I shouldn't bother
with kin.

Impossible.

My role, in this incarnation, is to preside over the affairs
of my relatives. It is fitting that we assemble.
Family is the pillar of the deme.

My own madness lies in wanting to travel with my siblings
to all points of a star,
in seeing how far they will wrench me
before I rend.

I am powerless when tempering my devotion.

I dream of us descending Mount Olympus
    holding hands,
        step-dancing
            and laughing.

    A bolt of unbroken white silk
            undulates overhead.

Turning Point

The strait stretches its dense indigo muscle:
            at its surface, concealed excitement
                        closer to the coast, patches of oily calm
                                    at its edges—waves like fingers gently stroking
                                    a forehead.

Marram Grass remains inert in the thin wind.
Yet the harbour crows sound distraught—
            squabbling over something that's been left unsaid.

Today is a semi-colon
                        a period for the sentence that was found
                                    a comma
                                                for what remains buried.

2.

Dear Kim

I left my art class and made my way down Powell Street. That March morning, my teacher had stopped at my easel and spoken to me about seeing. Now, the silver maple lurched toward me. As I searched its naked filigree for lines, palmate leaves wafted towards me (though they were not there). And then

flush with pigments and crosshatching, my body loosened its envelope and dispersed. Windborne, my presence extended—like a dandelion's parachute seeds—to the horizon's lost edges. My ribs became branches, the sky's blue my bloodstream. A revelation

strobed through me: bodies, by their very nature, nail us to solitude. Without expression, the world is an interconnected symmetry, and we stand at its centre. I hope I am not enraging you with this triviality. Cancer desolates you with outrageous lesions, swells your svelte limbs into grotesque appendages. Cancer's agony

steals you away. But I want you to know that rid of my body's confused loneliness, for a moment I became ecstatic and content.

Ill-Prepared

She has become a self-portrait, perched
temporarily
on the floor, immobile against
a taupe wall.

With the stoic frankness
of Frida Kahlo, she shows the crown
of bare skin atop her head—

from radiation before the bone-
marrow transplant—halo-like.

The refurbished living room now
contains a hospital
bed. She nestles
a small knapsack close
to her—inside, her self-
administered pain pump.

During my short time away, a vulgar
maroon-black rash has ravaged her left cheek,
chewed up half her left ear.

This illness is lasting too long—
her words are guttural:
Amélie's wedding, how can I go looking
like this?

I don't know
how to hold her
today.

The cliché *You must live in the now* comes to mind.
It stays in my mouth.

When I leave
she is angry
at me: she will be too busy for my visits.

On the bus
I receive a text: *I love you.*

Human Skin as an Explanation of What Happened to Her

Love particles are symmetrical and reach
all dimensions of a continuous surface. A mother might

insulate by interdigitating the children with toxic family history.
This is achieved through

unpredictable lashing out, scolding, slapping, and favouring one
sibling over the other. These behaviours bombard

the skin with short pulses which unnerve the papillary dermis; the irritation
spreads to the arteriovenous plexus

and confuses
the cellular machinery. A ripe environment now

exists for
self-loathing

to embed into the hypodermal tissue. The anatomical barriers against
the nurturer are determined by

the thickness of the child's skin. This daughter's temperament

was open to beauty and therefore particularly vulnerable. Once chaos
had burrowed

the belief—*I am bad*—was irrevocable and could not be altered.

The subsequent despair
(*je ne suis pas bien dans ma peau*)
breached the immune system and blinded
it,
refused to control cellular growth.

Family Inheritance

Was I altered
when Kim (like a daughter to me)
patted the hospital sheets
with her left hand
hours before
she would receive the injection?

When isolation-
room beeps were obliterated
by the exalted
summons of a thirty-year-old?

Did I hear spring
rustling through freshly sprouted catalpa leaves?

My mother wants to know

if Kim's cancer
reminds me
of my own cancer at thirty

how I fared
that weekend

was I able to make my way home

with my resolve
still intact.

Aftershocks

She is a day

gone by, as I slide into sleep

benevolence
found under the trees gathered in the gulley

she is absence—

the missing salt in pureed potatoes

the displaced edges of the old city

the tar-dock crows of my childhood

she is my surprise

on the bus by a young woman's back,
tuque
angled—*I'm walking here*

she is the lingering

smell of dill from last night's veal stew

she is the fountain pen's dried ink on a thank you note

she is my resolve

to stop my dismemberment
every time someone dies.

I Begin to Understand This Life Without Her

I shudder under hand-quilted
cotton as a knife trounces
the chopping-board
in quick succession (for chicken?)

whack!   whack!   whack!

I could risk shedding my coverings
to check on who might
be besieged at 3 am—
but I can't face a raw exchange
with family—

how I felt when Kim fixed
her see-though eyes on me (a habit
that started in her early 20s) before describing
one of my behaviours. She'd watch
as I shifted positions, crossed my arms.
She would then go quiet,

as if she knew this was my ceiling
of intimacy—
for now.

                As a child, she ran
                up Fault-Hill
                then disappeared
                behind it.

I Have No Home Here

It is not enough to hold the card
that says you love me, not enough
to imagine you as a vibrant thirty-year old

with children in tow; there are whiteouts
in Ottawa today and you are in a place outside
the landscape. I cannot reach it.

I read the spaces between your *sooner than later.*
They vibrate next to the wedge
of heart my mother left there. How life

taunts us this way, how I fail to snatch
its essential lessons. But your message—
I peel away its layers, visualize

a flower, drawings that you would like.
These days I lose nothing. Everything
remains the same. Yet, I know I have given all away.

3.

First Day in Sept-Iles

I turn the key, enter
the four-digit security code
three intermittent beeps …
all is clear.

My brother's ranch-style house is shrouded
in his family's absence, its echoes
almost tangible. I pull curtain drawstrings,
crank window handles

and the cathedral ceiling fills
with light.

The cedars edging the front walk
infiltrate the rooms with their fragrance.

I'm an intruder.

Everything I own is packed and stored.

I have no crisis.

My error: a belief that others
have a better life
(which constantly compels me to leave
mine behind).
You may not know
the mind that derides
past choices.

You may not know those existences—
landing strips of madness
that offer zero options.

You are then blessed, perhaps even a little happy.

The window in my brother's living room
follows the roofline's downward slope
as if finding its way to groundedness;
a perpendicular beam intercepts its inclination.

My nephew and his wife invite me for dinner.
After dessert, their son rests next to me,
iPad in hand, and shows me Bobble videos.

Daniel's closeness intensifies the gulf
            that surrounds me.

His small head is heavy on my arm
yet I do not move.

Blanketed in nightfall, I push the key
          shove the door open, search for light switches

and
        glance into the dark
             that shades the corner
                    of each room.

Soon knuckles tap on kitchen counter
a chair scrapes the floor, a pipe strikes metal.

The house is acclimatizing itself
to a change in temperature, I tell myself—

to a stranger's presence.

Unwritten

Some people carry a story, a story
they fabricated about themselves that they return to
for comfort. They understand
its exactitude.

I fear desire,

the sky awash in threat,
the pastel blue strip that suggests
indecision.

Clover, a scent from my childhood,

                                        (a poem must be free, able to scuttle
                                        over shiny wooden decks,
                                        risk getting tossed overboard)

long slow rumbles spread to the sky's edges.

I avoid walking to the Bay
                                        its archipelago
                    too daunting
from these shores.

A Trick of the Light

François and Kim glare at me from the Bay's mouth

the gulf alerts me   *they are both dead*

and I regain composure.

Papa drove us here when I was twelve
to see my mother's twin brother

Côte Nord's rain cramming us
in Uncle's Joe's bungalow.

From a black and white photo, my cousin François—ten,
his arm over my shoulders, mine
over his, both beaming   oblivious
to sisters, brothers, parents also posing
the two of us surprised in that moment
by the camera flash

that now, looking back
flared
through to our future
—the same city,
the same Sunday afternoons,
his eldest, Kim,
like a daughter to me.

Chromatic patterns that preserve
strange beauty.

Summer Solstice

The sun, spectacular at its highest point, longest day, blessing the hours and what is ours, summer stretching out like a cat, midsummer song, a lilt dedicated to Sol, hotter than anyone wants to admit (who doesn't love what burns?)

solstice, from *sol*, sun

symbolized in disks, circles with wings, rays, a human face harking back to Helios, a cross within the ring for the four seasons, to include all, symbols that let people go beyond the seen, express a way to stand in the world

solstice, from *sistere*, to stand still

a place to stand, but not here, notwithstanding clause, the earth deviating from the vertical, the world listing towards its limits, in the direction of, losing its ability to stand, then to be still, to let stillness come, to pause as it recoils, to supplicate.

Daniel, Almost Four

He expects plain answers.
I start with the tip of a tree branch, stop at the bud
that tucks tight into the limb.

Daniel leaves his Fisher-Price tool box
open on the grass, urges me towards
another tree, doesn't understand
why I am not instinctively moving
in his direction. He spills out
a slew of words which his excitement
enjambs.

I look quizzically at him. Earnestness
lines his forehead. He will fight
with every inch of his being
to have me understand that the world
I pretend exists, as I play with him

does exist.

He tries to reside within
the small globe of patience he owns.

He is fixing Planet Earth.

He pulls out a screwdriver from his kit.
Interrupting his concentration would be blasphemous.

As I watch him, a small part of me
is repaired.

Baie des Sept-Îles

Contemplate flight
at the edge
of the dock, let
yourself

melt, letting go
is gentle
remorse, allow
what is

bidden
to break
shore, your torpor
not warranted

the Bay's sheen aches to swallow
your plunge.

Home

Home is where you keep your boots
on, leave chocolate chip cookie crumbs behind,

rock to Heartbreak
Hotel

  because the absence
  of home makes you

melancholic when you venture too far beyond.

Home is where everything is
forgiven,

  the maroon terrycloth housecoat
  that envelopes like a blanket,

  the straw yellow pottery mug,

the mindless
TV.

  Home is the jade green end table
  you will never discard,

the slice of daybreak splitting
shade

and sill. Home is the shelf
where you store yourself,
where you've tried too hard,
or not at all.

  Home is where you suffer
  what is too much,

the too much
        that's never enough.

4.

Repointing the Bricks

Stop! Let me close the windows
but it's too late

a fine-powder dust
rushes through screens.
Inside, my house
is a white-faced Geisha

in mute submission
where I wipe floors, chairs, dressers,
picture frames, and the Raku tea bowl
on my knees.

These last months, the music

is all wrong.

My house exhales
its imperium
over me, damning my days
with blistered ceilings, warped
floors, cracked foundation.

My nights sink
into the Maple's taproot,
disturbing ancestors who hold my head
(as only the deceased can do)
between their forearms.
There, there.

Once my Blue Grotto,

my house has become a brawling
bouncer, bullying me out its door.

Undertow

A *For Sale* sign
banners my front yard.
Further down the small incline,
a picnic table under snow,
blue spruce wrapped in burlap.

I want to catapult
away from the inevitable
compression of days
that remain—
staying, I'll drift
in the opposite
direction of time.

How can I live without
the view of Dow's Lake?

But I'm fed up
watching myself in wicked
frustration, harassing roofers,
chasing electricians,
unable to right
the ill-mitered bank account.

I could learn to balance out the ends.

Whatever happened
to those years I worked towards
becoming a saint—
diving the Northumberland's surf
as I keened the day's blessings:
the smell of tarred docks
the blue herons silhouetted
at low tide. I did not need these walls
to anchor me in the illusion of belonging.

No complines will alleviate the nonsense:
this decision threatens
to leave me
behind.

Outside, the snow.

High Priest

The real estate agent straddles the entrance
with a door mat in each hand: *From Costco.*
He sets the Platinum Charcoal
carpet down, then the Herrington Grey,
tilting his head and pausing. He shimmies
the doormat that fits best in place, smiles.
To keep the house clean—
people will track dirt.

He accompanies me through
my home, counselling on its purification:
It's best to remove any personal traces.

When, about to sign
the listing document,
I hear
a death knoll—
he gives
a comforting nod:
I'm on your side.

I tell him that the vinyl runner
he placed at the entrance
is a burial pall over my life as I know it.

He tilts his head in empathy, cups my elbow:
This house stages beautifully.

Moving Day

is a quiet breath

I take in
this hour

wait to dispel
the house's shadow
but it won't leave

I tried shouting it
from the U-Haul boxes piled
high against moonlight-white
walls, my life raw
as the raucous holler
from a street reveller

I've been here before—
a decade ago—
everything sold
heirlooms spread

when my then husband
stood in the hallway,
blonde hair spraying
the black air
disturbing
the rud of open
truth that muscles
itself into houses

he—ensconced among Silver Maples
on a hilltop overlooking the river

I—entangled in that in-between state
of *what-ifs* and *if-onlys*
coiled around the need
to be held together.

Le puits

On the ledge flanking the well
my brother and I stand
as they lower a ten-gallon can
outside the summer kitchen

my brother and I stand
morning splashes us in yellow
outside the summer kitchen
my hand, like a cap's brim

morning splashes us in yellow
water at the bottom keeps milk cool
my hand, like a cap's brim
we call the old well *le puits*

water at the bottom keeps milk cool
Maman worries—stay away from the pit
we call the old well *le puits*
a weather-beaten wooden trapdoor

Maman worries—stay away from the pit
banishes *le puits'* rasping depth
a weather-beaten wooden trapdoor
we never fall in

banishes *le puits'* rasping depth
some mornings the hatchway gapes open
we never fall in
my limbs ache, too heavy to raise

some mornings the hatchway gapes open
I hear people in the summer kitchen
my limbs ache, too heavy to raise
sing praise for August lobster

I hear people in the summer kitchen
laugh over bowls of drawn-butter
sing praise for August lobster
they dip their shellfish

laugh over bowls of drawn-butter
I hide bad decisions
they dip their shellfish
my life's stone reserve

I hide bad decisions
some mornings the flap flings wide
my life's stone reserve
open, I imbibe purple-field-clover

as they lower a ten-gallon can
on the ledge flanking the well.

How to Live in a New Apartment

Open all the windows and let the rain stain floors.

Stand in the lobby and offer residents a poem.

Exchange verbs: *I want to ride my book.* It will improve elevator conversation.

Avoid building-managers: they shuffle days like cards and scramble time signals.

Wake at four a.m. and write down your ideas of the new world.

Stay away from the party room: here, there is too much nourishment and not enough glory.

Remember that whatever you imagine life to be, pebbles along the roadside are lies to be run over by cars. Replant them on your balcony. Every morning, unearth one and warm it in your hands.

393 Bell

There is no future
to this past
address, it takes me nowhere
but to an old apartment.
On the balcony
floor, a pigeon has enfolded itself
in a stillness
that alarms me.

At night
skin cells threaten
to go rogue. At night
generosity consoles
the part of me that insists
on remorse.

On the East Coast
the moon blankets the Northumberland's
worried depths.
If you brave the shock of callous cold
then liquid silver will stalk
the direction you swim in
and move your limbs so admirably that even

stillness
becomes a victory.

Minudie

A gunman in Nova Scotia, 22 dead,
a CBC camera pans
                                        the idyllic azure of Fundy Bay
                                        the Acadian dykes

and like a child scared by a dream
memory steps forward:

            I am ten, in the back seat of my parents' '49 Chevy
            marsh grasses sloping
            into a napping blue Chignecto Bay—

                        Minudie

            the woman we visit, a distant cousin
                        John William à Joseph à Olivier …
            her hair like dandelion-parachutes
                        in the lap of fields Acadians tilled
            her kitchen is the belly of a whale
            a window cuts a square of sun
                        displaced, you don't belong here

            on her knees, behind cupboard doors
            her hands tremble, she pulls out
            Queen Elizabeth II tins
            pops them open to offer us
            molasses cookies   iced cakes

sometimes it is not possible to complete the story

            there are peaches—
            Aunt Lorraine flips the can, makes a face
            shows me its rusted underbelly

from Minudie, to Shemogue, to—
John William, my grandfather—
Cap-Pelé

October Sunday, *Papa* at the wheel
bays narrowing into bays
dykes that gated tides
fall behind

we are safe

green salty air

land that never lets go.

Reality

Poetry is an affair of sanity, of seeing things as they are.
—Philip Larkin

Only one light-value captures reality's true expression. Reality can therefore appear flat or fearful and pleading to be refuted.

The scale and placement of the first shapes you see as a child can alter your light-grasp. When your childhood darkens the present, you are seeing wrong. Shift your eyes back from your current viewpoint to an instance you remember. This helps to balance and control the shadings of the past and to push it to a vanishing point.

Exaggerating incidents, due to tedium or the need to self-promote, sheds more light on an event than it should. Visualize an imaginary frame around the episode to locate its edges. Crop out irrelevant details.

To register a complex occurrence, picture it as a collection of contrasts adjacent to one another. Examine areas where shared boundaries with people cloud the spectrum; revisit those relationships.

Avoid using your mind to define what you observe: doing so risks bending light to fit a preconceived notion instead of distinguishing truth. A luminescent glow emanating from a lover's head is likely machination.

Seduction or wanting existence to be perfect blocks reality's candescence; illness or talking to a shrink who doesn't indulge your fabrications will intensify it.

The goal is to read every instance of reality's genuine brightness and thus gain proportion and perspective. There are no tricks. Doing so leads to a more easeful and peaceful life. You might even gain confidence in your ability to create a better composition, the world seemingly rearranging itself around you.

Ocean

Ocean's O swallows, an open mouth
best countered with quietness:

an inner mechanism that mimics wave action
and sneaks in a trail of letters
from a remote part of the city,
an ecosystem of ideas
thriving in semi-enclosed passages
that wake into open sea.

(see also: *creativity*)

A person may regain their voice
by placing both feet flat on wet sand
(avoid outer-foot coverings)
allowing the vector pattern
to acquaint them with the incalculable.

Caution: when it comes
to your bearings,
craving is equidistant from fear.

To soothe dread, head east and follow the sequence of dots
on the horizon. Eventually they will transfigure
into intermittent blinking
almost as if to say, extreme solitude
can only be palatable when pitted
against connection.

A Swimmer's Interruption

Fanned blades of parakeet green
jut through Wellington's
dim-grey asphalt.

I stand on a narrow bank,
stare into glass-clear aquamarine water—

sun-appointed eely shadows
rush its untainted seafloor.

I want to plunge
into the depths

where there's no return
once in.

Here, mollusks interrupt the tranquil sand.

Behind me,
someone watches
through a kitchen window.

I have managed to please them somewhat.

Edit Dream

Day
exclaims itself
cloud-brush on water-blue sky.

Meditate, stretch
tread purposefully in known places
until a friend trips you:
enough with your whining
success requires effort.

In isolation, day falls

an Operating Room
that exposes
flaw
mistake
without guile.

So, examine the beating heart
extract the lie
edit the dream
decide if you've suffered enough
find the source of the Northumberland
divert your course
heal, along with the planet
at excruciating speeds.

In a Time of Plague

While we're drawn to return to shallow time,
a new version of memory exists—
inhabited with talking dogs, watchful trees.
Day converts into a Möbius loop, and we trudge
its unoriented sand-paper surface.
Chests collapse in their struggle to find a beat,
anything that demarks completion. It is a sad time
for delineation. With yesterday's noise clap
out of bounds, tomorrow is overdue—
even if it rings hollow.
Let's have a rewrite.
Cast the future in a more forgiving light,
proffer a second chance
to mourn the air—Alleluia's tempo.

Madame Robson Predicts the Apocalypse

She broke into fourth grade math class,
wooden crucifix in hand.
Our teacher folded her arms,
looked down, stepped aside.

Madame Robson—long retired—
appeared this way, unannounced,

            and traced an arc in the air
            with the cross.

Pulling an embroidered hanky from her sleeve,
            she wiped the sides of her mouth
            before saying:

            The end of the world is here.

Her words sprayed:

            We are bad people.
            And now, Moncton
            is running out of water.

As I ran home for lunch,
I promised God
that I would stop fighting with my brother.

When I entered the kitchen,
Bernard stood at the sink,
looking intently up at our mother,
his face flushed.

Madame Robson had also visited *la veille école*,
where he attended.

Maman quickly dispelled our doom.
I'm not sure how.
She held truth.

Plates of cream-peas-on-toast
    alongside slices of ham
    steamed at the table.

We sat and wolfed down the meal
    without knowing
    our damnation would someday return.

The Sun Will Burst Through the Clouds in a Matter of Minutes

La vieille église was like an old piano—
out of tune and missing a few ivories.

Across the street, *l'église Sainte-Thérèse*'s
            imposing stone
            and gothic undertones
supplanted it.

On that June afternoon,
la vieille église swarmed with screaming children
gathered to watch *Tarzan's Fight for Life*
on a makeshift screen.

Just as Futa hypnotizes Moto into murdering Jane
the Petitcodiac river released a slow rumble
and white light flashed through the hall—then
lamp-black darkness
            a crashing deluge against wooden roof.
Grey metal chairs tumbled
as children ran zigzag across warped floors—
their faces flushed, hair wet with perspiration
breathless and hoarse

            The end of the world is here.

Molten fear jumped into my body.
I fought my way through to the foyer
and with uncommon strength
heaved against the large church door.

            I would swim home.

Dream to Dream

The snap
of cotton bedsheets billowing in the wind
awakens me, I rise in the sweltering night
and from my 7th floor perch
I watch a mob advance on Wellington street—
the front of a tidal bore—
grim bridal march,
grey water-logged garments drooping
from their shoulders like seaweed.
They hold Japanese anemones, a red rose,
brandish the world's empty promise in their pocket squares.

On those first nights,
tones of re-claimed
breath wafted up

into the clammy air,
harmonized
into plainsong.

I hid from the walkers,
believing their death
was somehow contagious.

I'm not equipped to tell love stories,
though I once was. I had no idea then
what was held within the source
of love, thinking it was boundless,
that I would come upon
something even more perfect
in due time. Now I wonder how
I'll live on, why love stands outside us.

I wash away the plague
with salt bottled from the Red Sea;
fear of contagion
with cornmeal from my grandmother's pantry.

Opening my balcony door I breathe in
the kind of afternoon
I used to pick blueberries in low fields;
looking up
I imagine Northumberland's own
version of blue. Those days
were full of firmament, ocean,
and periwinkle berries hidden under boughs.
Enough blues to supply a life's worth.

Later, the night marchers'
chants transmute
into an extended compass
of notes that moves me
from dream to dream.

The anxiety of being held
by a single syllable abates.

As the processions increase
the dead wander into day,
pass by ICU nurses
who stand straight up,
arms crossed, face masks on, silent.

I amble into a shop, buy Crispin
apples that I slice up for pie.

Rain in Ottawa

For hours, alone on a red clay PEI
road, I heave my dead-weight feet.
Overhead, to my right—low battleship
clouds, their underbellies
injected with a coulee of blood.
I need to warn Kim …
I speed-dial her number, over and over.
All I hear is an unresponsive, metallic
buzz tone.

I wake up
to rain.
It is 4 am.

Kim's death is with me even
in this new apartment, no way through
or around layers of opaque curtains
lining towering casements

I try to recall the colour-pencil self-portrait
she sketched at ten
the dome-shaped eyelids, the repeated arcs that built bangs
her confident lines full of excitement

come morning
I vow to stroll along Dow's Lake's boardwalk
let the surface-frisson
spur me into walking straighter

through the open window, solitary footsteps—
a light clacking of stiletto heels against sidewalk.

Acknowledgements

"Bio," "The Dune as Bookmark," "Lion's Mane Jellyfish," "Turning Point," "Human Skin as an Explanation of What Happened to Her," "Family Inheritance," "I Begin to Understand This Life Without Her," and "I Have No Home Here" first appeared in the chapbook, *The Dune as Bookmark*, published by Anstruther Press in 2019.

I am deeply grateful to my family and friends for their long-standing support of my writing.

I am fortunate to be part of the Ruby Tuesdays, a writing group whose poets motivate and inspire me through their example.

For his encouragement, counsel, and impeccable editing acumen, I am profoundly indebted to Jim Johnstone.

And finally, my heartfelt thanks to Denis De Klerck at Mansfield Press for giving me the great honour of publishing this collection.

Jacqueline Bourque grew up along New Brunswick's ocean shores. She spent the better part of her career in Ottawa working as a communicator in the public sector. Her poetry has been featured in a number of journals and anthologies including *The Fiddlehead, The Antigonish Review, Queen's Quarterly, The Dalhousie Review*, and *I Found It at the Movies*. In 2019, she released a chapbook titled *The Dune as Bookmark*, published by Anstruther Press. *Repointing the Bricks* is her debut collection.